"Philosophy of education is not just the
a curriculum, a body of proven yet der
*Republic* and Rousseau's *Emile* to Dewey
*tion*. Novice teachers are often unprepared to take such works
on board. They are more likely to resist them, to regard them as
senseless intrusions upon their practical training. Every teacher
of philosophy of education feels this tension. Rocha addresses
it directly in this work, which is written specifically for our students as our fellows. Through this little book he welcomes them
into a friendly conversation and makes them feel at home. This
is not yet the conversation of philosophy, as Rocha makes crystal
clear. It is a preliminary conversation, a "primer"—an undercoat
to prepare students to receive the further layers of philosophical
text and reflection that constitute philosophy of education. This
is a necessary kind of book and to my knowledge, no one before
Rocha has written one like it."

—LEONARD J. WAKS

PROFESSOR EMERITUS, TEMPLE UNIVERSITY

"Too few today who talk about education have much to say in
this regard, and, in contradistinction to one of Rocha's most
important statements, reduce education to schooling. This is a
depraved reduction, which demands a forceful response. And
it is in this way that we should read Rocha's primer: as chan-
neling that force of the philosophical tradition that, in one moment, takes us by the hand and shows us the grand possibility of
thinking, and, in the next, takes us by the scruff of our necks and
insists that we go public with the fearless speech that philosophy
has given us. The tradition of philosophy is renewed, again, with
this book and so many efforts like it that are happening in a time
when education is deprived of thinking, and dare I say, with Rocha, love of wisdom."

—EDUARDO M. DUARTE

PROFESSOR, HOFSTRA UNIVERSITY

"What a sweet teacher Sam Rocha is. Like a patient parent, he explains and inspires. Teach this book!"

—WILLIAM F. PINAR

PROFESSOR AND CANADA RESEARCH CHAIR,
UNIVERSITY OF BRITISH COLUMBIA

"To prime education's philosophy is to invite us all to begin again, again . . . and again. Priming one's life is a daily occurrence by which we always seek to live by learning and unlearning what we do and what we are. It is in this recognition of doing and being that we educate ourselves as each other's others; as a society of free, intelligent and equal human beings. What *A Primer for Philosophy and Education* adds to this daily occurrence is the lyricism of meaning by which love and being reach each other on the daily thresholds of normality."

—JOHN BALDACCHINO

CHAIR OF ARTS EDUCATION, UNIVERSITY OF DUNDEE

"A charming and clearly written introduction to the philosophy of education, inspired by the writings of William James."

—GRAHAM HARMAN

PROFESSOR OF PHILOSOPHY,
THE AMERICAN UNIVERSITY IN CAIRO

"This is an excellent little work, a minor opus. It achieves exactly what it ought to achieve: it makes me want to start this journey. It makes me aware of my own philosophy, my own love of wisdom. The illustrations are whimsical, and seriously so."

—SETH EINTERZ

STUDENT, GEORGETOWN UNIVERSITY SCHOOL OF MEDICINE

"*A Primer for Philosophy and Education* provides students with a surprisingly comprehensive glimpse into the philosophy of education. The book is a personal invitation to join Sam Rocha in a discussion about the philosophy of language, conceptual analysis, epistemology and metaphysics, and consider each area's application to education. He effectively shows students philosophy of education rather than merely telling them about the subject. This is a remarkable introduction to the field from an imaginative and gifted author."

—EMERY HYSLOP-MARGINSON
PROFESSOR AND CHAIR, FLORIDA ATLANTIC UNIVERSITY

"In a delightful little book with wonderful illustrations and a direct intimacy with his audience, Sam Rocha in deceptively simple language engages the reader with a primer that covers a range of topics from philosophy and education to Cordelia, things, language, courage, knowledge and understanding, and being in love. Highly recommended."

—MICHAEL A. PETERS
PROFESSOR OF EDUCATION, UNIVERSITY OF WAIKATO

"Rocha creates a canvas on which philosophy and education speak to a modern generation. He gives education a good name in every sense of the word and is a motivation for up and coming enthusiasts who want to be teachers."

—MATT POPNOE
RETIRED SCIENCE TEACHER, BRADY HIGH SCHOOL

"Sam Rocha's *Primer* is something I've literally never seen before. It's a little book that is ostensibly about education and philosophy and really is about those things, not about theories or methods. No single sentence or page in this primer was earth-shattering; it all seemed familiar, if vaguely so. But like all truly innocent things, this little book left me shattered. It reminded me, gently and simply, that I had forgotten the purpose of life, the way to go about it, and why it matters. Rocha's little primer ends as innocently as it begins: with an admonishment for the reader to be in love. "Love alone is sufficient for all things," Rocha says. But what could elsewhere be mistaken for a saccharine Hallmark observance here has the force of a punch. This is a book everyone should read, whether you're a university student or a hairdresser or a high school football player. It is a primer for philosophy and education, at their most basic levels. As such, it's really a primer for life."

—CALAH ALEXANDER
MOTHER AND WRITER

"In the pages of this text, Sam Rocha has written a patient and personal letter to, among others, students new to philosophy and education. Rocha's voice is reassuringly clear as he encourages an engagement with a grand yet inescapable enterprise. Those already initiated will surely recognize the wisdom of Rocha's careful approach as they recall their own experiences preparing students for similar studies. Rocha reminds us of our shared and very special duty to prepare our students well for the often surprising, confounding, and richly fulfilling work ahead."

—WINSTON C. THOMPSON
ASSISTANT PROFESSOR, UNIVERSITY OF NEW HAMPSHIRE

"Sam Rocha has written a rare book about philosophy and education. This is a book for beginning philosophers, which is to say it is a book for all of us. It is also a book for beginning teachers, and the best of teachers are always beginning, always returning to their roots and sources of inspiration. It is both simple and demanding. Rocha shows how both philosophy and education demand rigorous attention to fundamentals upon which to grow."

—TIMOTHY LEONARD
PROFESSOR EMERITUS, ST. XAVIER UNIVERSITY

"Sam Rocha is a bold, insightful, and original voice in philosophy of education, and these qualities shine through in his engaging *A Primer for Philosophy of Education*. It is an excellent resource for students new to education, but also for veterans, as Sam helps all see the familiar in a new way."

—KEVIN GARY

CHAIR AND ASSOCIATE PROFESSOR OF EDUCATION, GOSHEN COLLEGE

"Sam Rocha's *A Primer for Philosophy and Education* provides readers with reflections about philosophy and education from the vantage point of an artist and musician. It provides a helpful way forward for educators and students alike to reflect on the construction of a personal philosophy about learning and a philosophy of education in general. The primer adroitly uses the metaphor of painting to the work of crafting a philosophy of education and for reflection about learning. Rocha draws the reader in through personal narrative about the creative process and how it can be a liberating force in the development of philosophical insights. The primer is a summons to not only engage in philosophy or education, but to think concretely about the telos of philosophy and education itself."

—PAUL MYHRE

ASSOCIATE DIRECTOR,
WABASH CENTER FOR TEACHING AND LEARNING IN THEOLOGY AND RELIGION

"Sam Rocha's *Primer* is an absolutely unique text that manages to pull the reader into a new world. Once you have started reading, it is impossible to stop before you are finished. Rocha's feat is to write a short text which, at the end, gives a feeling of having undertaken an infinitely long journey. All the way there is encouragement for reflection, that is, a loving kind of reflection that strives for wisdom. Due to its distinctive style, the primer is a rare work, but the hope is that there will be more such works in the genre of philosophy of education."

—HERNER SAEVEROT

PROFESSOR OF EDUCATION, UNIVERSITY OF BERGEN

"More often than not, philosophical primers come in one or two forms. First, there is the primer that is dedicated to teaching the fundamentals of argumentation and reasoning. Second, there are a variety of primers on philosophers and philosophers of education which give basic biographical details, collect insightful excerpts from their work, and end with guiding questions to facilitate class discussion. Rocha has presented us with a third, highly unique option. For him, a primer is not about cultivating a set of skills or about providing background information. Rather the primer primes the student for a philosophical experience. Through a mix of personal stories, highly imaginative prose, and playful metaphors, Rocha presents the primer as an opening to being philosophical. Thus to prime oneself means, on the level of embodiment, relaxing, and, on the level of the mind, opening up and being receptive. Philosophy here is not simply learning about rules for formulating arguments. Nor is it acquiring information about what philosophers in the past have said. It is rather about understanding why anything is anything at all through careful, attentive description. But in the end what the primer primes the student for is neither philosophy nor education but for love. Rocha concludes with a passionate plea that at their most basic level education and philosophy are united in romantic entanglement through the love of wisdom. Any student who reads this primer will be inspired to love the world, and through this love become educated."

—Tyson Lewis

Associate Professor, University of North Texas

"What a gift! Sam Rocha's *Primer* not only takes the pedagogue's fundamental, most ethical step of declaring to students and to the world what [his] philosophy of education is, but the author does so in a didactic and loving way that much resembles the prophetic voice of Brazilian educator Paulo Freire. Rocha's invites students who first encounter the subject of education in academic settings to take responsibility for thinking and knowing as a pre-conditional act for those concerned with the moral implications of affecting in conscious, deliberate ways the teaching and learning of others"

—SANDRO BARROS

ASSOCIATE PROFESSOR OF MODERN LANGUAGES, DEPAUW UNIVERSITY

"Sam Rocha's *Primer* is a strong example of the strength of the performative, a piece that at once lays out a vision for philosophy and education and accomplishes that vision in the telling. Although presumably a primer for the introductory courses he teaches, Rocha's *Primer* deftly negotiates key themes in philosophy that echo his Jamesian leanings about the centrality of things, wisdom, and love. Couched in straightforward language yet retaining the tone and tenor of his field, Rocha manages to deliver an introduction of a philosophy of education that critiques contemporary schooling and serves as a call to action for a return to understanding education as a love of knowing and being known."

—WALTER S. GERSHON

ASSOCIATE PROFESSOR, KENT STATE UNIVERSITY

"*A Primer for Philosophy and Education* is not the usual introductory textbook. It won't introduce you to the common issues in philosophy of education. Rather it is a book that will prepare you for such issues. It is a book about the attitudes and passions that sincere philosophizing and education requires. Rocha not only speaks about such attitudes and passions, but also writes with such attitude, full of passion, with a sense of urgency. He demonstrates an intimate engagement with personal education and philosophy in its original form, as a love for wisdom. This is the kind of book every student of education and philosophy should begin to read and then come back to frequently. I most certainly will, both for myself and with my students. We all need to be reminded of primary love and courage that philosophy and education require of us."

—VIKTOR JOHANSSON

ASSISTANT PROFESSOR, DEPARTMENT OF CHILD AND YOUTH STUDIES,
STOCKHOLM UNIVERSITY

"Sam Rocha's primer reminds me of a French adage: *la philo descends dans la rue*—philosophy comes to the street. Rocha's little book can be read and talked about, with profit, on the street, in the home, in the school, in the garden, anywhere the human heart beats and the human mind thinks."

—DAVID T. HANSEN
WEINBURG PROFESSOR IN THE HISTORY AND PHILOSOPHY OF EDUCATION,
TEACHERS COLLEGE, COLUMBIA UNIVERSITY

"In this small book, Sam Rocha takes on the magnificent task of introducing us to the puzzling relationship between education and philosophy. He offers a measure, "no more and no less, and several imperatives, "be serious, brave, go after the truth of what is there, and dare to be in love." Sam Rocha allows us to learn in the book from many different teachers: from his grandfather and from his children, from a distance runner, from William James, from an artist and then from Shakespeare's Cordelia. As a reader of this book, one smoothly moves from preparing the self for the work of philosophy, to simply doing it. By inscribing himself in the tradition that views philosophy as a spiritual practice, Rocha gives us a compelling experience of first-hand philosophizing, in which the ordinary is shown in its powerful features, and the discipline of philosophy of education reclaims its necessity."

—CRISTINA CAMMARANO
ASSISTANT PROFESSOR OF PHILOSOPHY, SALISBURY UNIVERSITY

"An elegantly written invitation to students and the general reader to a frame of mind where one is ready to learn from and think about philosophy and education. Sam Rocha calls us all back, in heart-felt yet precise prose, to philosophy's ancient role of dialogue, wonder, and reflection. A joy to read and treasure."

—AG RUD
DISTINGUISHED PROFESSOR, WASHINGTON STATE UNIVERSITY

"Rocha's illustrated primer is an eye-opening introduction to the philosophy of education. And, unlike too many illustrated texts, its pen and ink drawings are a thought provoking complement to this highly readable introduction."

—DAVID MOSLEY

PROFESSOR OF PHILOSOPHY, BELLARMINE UNIVERSITY

What more is education than schooling? What more is philosophy than the knowledge philosophers? By exploring how education is synonymous with life itself, and philosophy with a kind of love, Sam Rocha illuminates how these two pursuits nourish understanding. In crystal clear, yet poetic language, he reminds us that what is at stake in them is nothing less than the possibility of joy. His marvelous primer is addressed not to experts or trainees, but to the soul in us all.

—RENE ARCILLA

PROFESSOR OF PHILOSOPHY OF EDUCATION,
STEINHARDT SCHOOL OF CULTURE, EDUCATION, & HUMAN DEVELOPMENT,
NEW YORK UNIVERSITY

# A Primer for Philosophy and Education

# A Primer for Philosophy and Education

## Samuel D. Rocha

 CASCADE *Books* · Eugene, Oregon

A PRIMER FOR PHILOSOPHY AND EDUCATION

Cascade Books
An Imprint of Wipf and Stock Publishers
199 W. 8th Ave., Suite 3
Eugene, OR 97401

www.wipfandstock.com

ISBN 13: 978-1-62564-922-5

*Cataloging-in-Publication data:*

Rocha, Samuel D.

A Primer for Philosophy and Education / Samuel D. Rocha.

xxviii + 54 p.; 21.5 cm.

ISBN 13: 978-1-62564-922-5

1. Education. 2. Philosophy.

LB885.R74.2014

Manufactured in the USA

*In loving memory of and gratitude for my abuelito,*
*Andrés Rocha.*

"…from the bottom of my heart it is all the same to me what the professional philosophers of today think of me; for it is not for them that I am writing."

—LUDWIG WITTGENSTEIN

# CONTENTS

# PREFACE TO
# THE SECOND EDITION

THIS BOOK BEFORE YOU, that began as an appendix to my course syllabus and grew into a self-published instructional text, has now become slightly different in scope and aspiration. My intent in writing it remains teacher-focused—this is a book for teaching—but it has acquired some clarity with regard to the range of its possibilities and applications.

This came as a surprise to me, through the use of, and interest in, its previous iteration. It has now appeared in homes, churches, middle and high schools, undergraduate institutions and graduate courses. It has been found suitable for general studies of many kinds, especially those situated within the humanities and liberal arts, most of all those that orbit religious, philosophical, and/or educational themes and concerns.

This unexpectedly broad reception indicated that certain changes needed to be made to be more hospitable to more audiences and readerships. I also realized, at the helpful suggestion of several colleagues, that some additions were needed, but not too many. Aside from this new preface, I've added questions, thoughts, and exercises to the end of each section and have included a list of suggested texts (including some music and film) for further study at the end.

These additions have enlarged the scope of this book. It has grown from being strictly instructional into something like a condensed curriculum for the philosophy of education, appropriate for use and adaptation by anyone able to read and understand it. The difference between instruction and curriculum is important to recognize because it indicates a slight, but fundamental, shift. Instruction is *given*, whereas a curriculum can only be *offered*.

One implication of this distinction is that I am in weaker possession of this text now than ever before, due in part to the enormous debts I have accumulated over the past three years of writing and editing it. There are so many people to thank, but my first thanks are to my students at Wabash College, for whom I first wrote it, and at the University of North Dakota. Michael Brown, Stephen Webb, Eduardo Duarte, Brad Rowe, Tim Leonard, Gary

Perkerwicz, Kathy Gershman, Mike Blaha, Andre Mazawi, Jennifer Milam, Justin Tse, my sister and illustrator, Ana Maria Rocha, and my wife, Anne Rocha, also offered invaluable love and support. Christian Amondson and the editorial board at Wipf and Stock have shown confidence in me and for that I cannot thank them enough. Of course, the usual disclaimer applies: all of its faults are my own.

August 2014—University of British Columbia
Vancouver, British Columbia, Canada

# PREFACE TO
# THE FIRST EDITION

I've written this little book with three audiences in mind. The first two are obvious: those reading it for a course I am teaching, and others reading it on their own. The third audience may seem strange, but is absolutely true, nevertheless: I am the third audience.

This primer has different things to show each of us, or different ways of showing the same things. I will try to speak to some of those differences here.

*To my students*—I wrote this primer for instructional purposes. This book is, first and foremost, a text written by a teacher to and for his students. You shouldn't wonder whether you have my full attention. I am not writing to you by accident or coincidence. I am not principally concerned with anyone else but you. This narrow, specialized focus should give you total confidence that you are the intended audience.

A major inspiration for this project comes from one of my favorite philosophers, William

James. One of the many things I've learned from him is to avoid the dangers of incestuous writing, writing within an echo chamber.

James wrote for more than the highly schooled, professional audiences of the academy. He wrote for them, too, but he didn't always write to or for an exclusive field of peers, due in large measure to the fact that he never belonged to a single field in the first place—he began in anatomy and physiology, moved to psychology, and ended in philosophy with major interests in religion and metaphysics.

Perhaps a better way to think about him is like this: James belonged to a field of study coincidentally, classified by whatever he was working on at the moment, but never limited by or to that classification.

James published mostly works of popular philosophy that began as lectures he presented to audiences of all kinds of people. He also frequently wrote essays, reviews, and letters to periodicals and popular journals, sometimes under the pseudonym "ignoramus." William James was a public intellectual in the most honorable sense; he had a deep sensitivity to what I call "pastoral philosophy"—an ordinary sense of philosophy that is thoroughly and principally educational.

As you will see in fuller detail, 'philosophy' and 'education' are different words for similar, if not the same, mysterious things. The terms should be taken as harmonious and complimentary.

My favorite set of essays by James, added to the end of his famous *Talks to Teachers on Psychology*, is titled *And To Students, on Some of Life's Ideals*. This trio of essays has been influential to me for many reasons. Most importantly, I was a graduate student when I first read them; these essays were penned *To Students*. To me. I took them personally.

Again and again in his essays, books, and correspondence, James took time to write specifically to and for his students.

For example, after the publication of his magisterial *The Principles of Psychology*, and at the height of his status as a psychological specialist, James published a shorter version of *The Principles*, for instructional purposes, titled *Psychology: The Briefer Course*. James aficionados have clever nicknames for each book: they call the first book "the James," and the second "the Jimmy."

Throughout his life, James showed a sensitive ability to move between "James" and "Jimmy," to write to students (and teachers) without compromising the integrity or rigor of his thought. I remain a student of James to this day. When I re-read him, I continue to find his voice powerful and intimate. Personal.

Following James, I want to be clear that it is you, the student, to whom I am writing. This book is for you. Feel welcome and at home in these pages. Live in them a little if you can.

This primer should acquaint you with what philosophy and education are to me, as far as I can understand them, and might become to you. It should also orient you to the disposition—the overall posture and attitude—that the work of philosophy and education require. I hope you refer to it as a practical resource you can use throughout the course. Use it well.

*To others*—As you surely know by now, this book was not principally written to or for you. I do not say this to try to exclude you outright. After all, one can be a student without being enrolled in a class or at a formal school. In a certain way of thinking, all readers are students as all authors are teachers. I became a student of Professor James by reading his books.

There is no reason to think of what I wrote in the previous section as somehow exclusive to those literally enrolled in my classes. To my potential and figurative students and inter-locutors, to my readers: the same aforemen-tioned spirit applies to and for you. The lines dividing my classroom from your own are not easily or neatly defined.

*To myself*—As I have edited and revised this project, I've developed another sense of purpose about it: I have also written it to re-mind and hold myself accountable to what philosophy and education are, are not, and might someday become.

In many ways, this short book holds all the bits and pieces of my previous work in the philosophy of education. This, again, under-scores the merit in seeing and understanding this book as an instructional, pedagogical text: by writing this primer for philosophy and education, I am simultaneously and ir-reducibly acting as philosopher and educator.

I hope to revisit and measure my future work by the sentiments and intuitions con-tained here. This is not to say that I will not change. It is instead to hope that what is pe-rennial to philosophy and education will en-dure, even as my thought (r)evolves.


April 2013—University of North Dakota
Grand Forks, North Dakota, USA

# INTRODUCTION

HAVE YOU EVER PAINTED something? If you have (and have done beautiful work) then you probably already know what a "primer" is.

For those who may not be so well acquainted: before you can properly paint a surface—before you can paint a car, a house, or a cabinet—you must first prime it. This involves all sorts of preliminary tasks: washing, scraping, sanding, and so on. Once the preliminaries have been executed, and executed well, the first thing that is applied to the readied surface is called

"primer." In a sense, one must "prime" the surface for priming! Get used to this Russian doll or onion-like, layered situation.

The priming process is preparatory but essential; it prepares a surface to become a base, receptive to the coats of paint that will follow. This is what the word 'primer' points to. This is what it attempts to describe and show. To be extra clear: the word 'primer' refers to the preparatory stage that enables the upcoming work to be done, and done well. You could paint without priming, but that would be cheap, second-rate work.

If you are going to be serious about your work, you must prime your surface. It is no joking matter. When I use the word 'serious' I am not trying to exclude leisure or humor. In some cases the serious thing to do is to relax. Someone who takes life too seriously is not being serious enough about it. To be serious about something is to take it as it is and treat it accordingly.

Imagine a distance runner who does not stretch, eat well, or hydrate her body before a marathon. This runner is a fraud and a phony, a poser; she is not serious and will not be competitive. She is unprepared. Do not be like this unprepared distance runner. Be serious. Prepare yourself. To be serious, you must be willing to work hard. If you are not serious about philosophy it will be hard to be serious about education, and vice versa. Serious runners must rest, too, but not too much. Excessive preparation would be equally unserious as not enough of it. In the same way, one cannot prime too much or forever. What is important here is not the priming itself; the craft of philosophy and education is what we are after.

If the labor and artistry of these intertwined crafts does not interest you, then you should certainly not begin. Disinterest breeds a lack of seriousness. Quit for now and go discover something about which you can be serious. Go paint a house or run a marathon. Learn and master a different, but equally worthwhile, craft.

When a piece of wood is properly primed, it becomes receptive to the paint that will follow. It is ready to absorb some of the paint, stain, or varnish; but it is not primed to do so without resistance. Think of a board as a sponge—a very hard, nonabsorbent sponge. Priming involves struggle and resistance. It is not passive. While it is important that you prepare yourself for the painting of

3

philosophy and education, I do not intend your preparation to preclude you for passivity or indoctrination.

A primed board is still resistant, allowing its surface to be painted, but nothing deeper. Not yet: only something much more potent, like fire, termites, or prolonged immersion in water, can pierce into its core. This should clarify what I am asking of you and, also, what I am not asking.

As you have seen, this primer for philosophy and education uses the expression 'primer' quite literally: it is intended to prepare you to become receptive, in the proper way, to the philosophical and educational content that will follow. It should help you avoid doing second-rate work. It will invite you to be serious about philosophy, education, and, hopefully, things in general: everything.

‡

A thought and a question: Think of a time you primed something. It doesn't have to be wood or your mind; it could be anything. What happened?

## 2

## PRIMING AND PAINTING

Priming can seem ironic. It can appear almost identical to painting because both are forms of brushing a substance onto a surface. As we've seen: after the preliminaries, primer is applied with a brush, in the same strokes as the paint to follow. In this sense, to "prime" is just to "paint"—to paint with primer. For this reason, priming and painting can become confused, although, in a certain way of seeing things, they might appear to be the same thing.

The difference, of course, is that there is a distinction, and a governing order, between brushing with primer ("priming") and brushing with paint ("painting"). For me to write and for you to study this book is to philosophize and educate, but there is a difference between philosophizing and educating "with primer" and philosophizing and educating "with paint." This book should accomplish both: prepare and perform.

For example, imagine that you are priming your wall for painting, and someone walks into the room. She could easily think you are painting, and who could blame her? You're holding a brush or a roller, dipping it into a pan of what appears to be paint, applying a different color to the wall—making it look different. When she asks what you are doing, you would be hard-pressed to say that you are not painting. But the truth would be more precise than this: you are priming in one sense and painting in another. The only sense in which you are painting is in the brushing, the external movements. The sequence and order of your work tells a more complete and delicate truth.

These are the complexities of a primer for philosophy and education: even while priming I may appear to be painting. The preparation is performative. Due to these ironies, you may feel a sense of frustration and absurdity while reading this primer. If you do, persevere. These feelings are natural to any work that is serious and worthwhile. Running a marathon, I am told, feels totally absurd and hopelessly frustrating—at the beginning.

‡

Some thoughts and questions: Think of two other cases where the preparation can seem identical to the performance. What are they? Why do they seem identical and in what ways are they distinct?

3

# EDUCATION AND PHILOSOPHY

Everyone comes into direct contact with education. Anyone willing to look can see that education is common, ordinary, and pertinent to all. No one can opt out of education. There are no dropouts. We're all educated in some way; we always have been and will be, no exceptions. To prove this, ask yourself these questions: Who is not educated in some way? When is education not going on? Where is education absent?

See?

We have been, are, and will be educated in various ways, throughout our lives. There are many kinds of education—explicit and implicit, conventional and unconventional, new and old, beautiful and ugly, familiar and bizarre, fair and unfair, good and evil—but the bare reality of education is singular and unavoidable.

For better and for worse, education happens constantly and indiscriminately. It's the water we're swimming in, the air we breathe. Like breathing, education usually happens without voluntary intent, consent, or attention.

Perhaps it is because of this ubiquity that people often feel more comfortable with the subject of education than philosophy. If you are a teacher or have been a student you may feel at ease with education because of your presupposed experience with it, while finding philosophy intimidating or confusing because it seems foreign and new.

To prime yourself for philosophy and education, I would ask you to consider the relationship between them in exactly the opposite way. You may soon discover that you have more conscious familiarity with philosophy than you do with education. This may seem strange, but it would simply be to realize that things are not always as they seem. In the end, I think you will come to find that you have been very intimate with both—even at the exact same time!

One thing you should recognize is this: when I use the word 'education' I am not exclusively referring to formal or compulsory schooling. I do not consider the terms 'education' and 'schooling' to be synonyms.

Education is not exclusively contained within a classroom or a building. Sure, education happens in schools, but it also happens everywhere else.

Education cannot be institutionalized or corralled. If you equate education with schooling, you may find this book very confusing. And if you are interested only in formal schooling, you may find it pointless and silly. However, if you care about the art of teaching, you will need to have more than schooling in your heart and mind. Beautiful teaching requires an explicit, philosophical interest in education—in the widest sense. A gifted teacher always sees more to things than the institution or the profession dictates. Any teacher worthy of the name sees the *person*. In this minimal sense we all can strive to be teachers; and for some of us, teaching is a vocation.

Again: Education cannot be domesticated. Because it is so wild and vast, education is particularly difficult to describe. Philosophy is much easier by comparison.

Perhaps this is the relevance of philosophy to education: philosophy helps us attempt to understand education. These philosophical attempts, in turn, educate us. And in being educated, we live out the work of philosophy. Education and philosophy complement each other.

‡

Some thoughts and questions: Think of at least three situations where you felt that you were educated—i.e., where you received an education of some kind—that did *not* take place in a school or a classroom. Where were you? What happened?

# 4

# PHILOSOPHY AND PHILOSOPHERS

To PRIME YOURSELF SPECIFICALLY for philosophy—a form of priming for, and painting with, education—you must first attend to the preliminaries. Prepare your mind. Wash it clean of any debris, scrape away as many needless pretensions and presuppositions as you can, sand the surface to a bare, receptive—but not too receptive, not empty—state. Examine yourself. Look for places that need preliminary treatment: Ego, books, the news, preferences and tastes, family, political and religious ideologies and pet theories. You cannot expect to do anything well without proper preparation, and philosophy is no exception.

If you are a newcomer to philosophy, if it is entirely unfamiliar to you, take hope: You are probably better suited to priming than those who are familiar with it. You have no baggage—no hard, calcified layers to scrape away. If you are comfortable with philosophy, be on guard. Many of your assumptions about philosophy may impede your ability to be primed for it.

Most of you are newcomers. I am not saying this to insult or patronize. I suspect that most of you are newcomers because most people nowadays do not study philosophy itself. They study philosophers. Most so-called philosophers these days do not write or teach philosophy. They write and teach about philosophers who, once upon a time, wrote and taught philosophy. Most work in philosophy happens second- or third-hand.

There is nothing wrong with this "handed down" kind of philosophy. Nothing is wrong with it, that is, until it is confused with first-hand, original philosophy. History is important. Biography too. It is simply a matter of keeping the proper order between different things—understanding the difference between a biography and an autobiography.

Do not shy away from reading philosophers (after all, you are reading one right now) or even philosophers writing about other philosophers. But do not confuse this with doing philosophy yourself, which in some cases will involve engaging with the thought of another philosopher. Never lose yourself unless you are doing it to find yourself.

To prepare for the philosophical portion of this priming, you must understand the difference between philosophy and philosophers. But do not to assume too much about what this difference entails. All I mean is this: There is an obvious difference between a poet and a scholar of poetry. Of course, the scholar of poetry may also, in addition to her scholarship, be a poet. Both roles are important, but each is distinct from the other in ways that should not be equated.

Do not be fooled into thinking that knowing a lot of trivia or data—such as bits and pieces of information about philosophers—amounts to a serious familiarity with philosophy. Erudition is not necessary for original philosophy.

There is a difference between the history of philosophy and the philosophy of history. At the very least, there is a difference in emphasis. The first (history of philosophy) is historical; it is an attempt to give an account of the ideas of the past. The second (philosophy of history) is philosophical; it is an attempt to think about what history is. Both have value and are worthwhile and even complimentary, but only one is principally philosophy.

Again, you will not need encyclopedic stores of authors and titles of books or specialized words and jargon. You will need only a clear, curious mind and a heart that is passionate and wild enough to sustain and feed a lively, probing imagination.

Don't ignore your emotions and desires, but know how to tell the difference between the petty ones and the magnificent ones, the ones that are serious and the ones that are not—and respond appropriately. Your desires to live, to understand, to fall in love are magnificent. Your more shallow feelings of comfort, self-esteem and the like are, usually, petty.

In other words, there are no special, exclusive, or extraordinary tools for philosophy. Philosophy is not the work of geniuses, magicians, virtuosos, or superhumans. You already have everything you need inside and all around you. There is no superstition to philosophy. There are no incantations. Everything is as ordinary as the world itself. Nonetheless, what is perfectly ordinary will surprise you from time to time as splendidly and terribly strange, perplexing, and mysterious!

The ordinary, when attended to closely and with care, is extraordinary all on its own—and we are educated by it.

‡

A thought and some questions: Think of another comparison that resembles the distinction I drew between philosophy and philosophers. What is it? How does it retain the aspects of my distinction between philosophy and philosophers?

# 5

## CORDELIA

SHAKESPEARE TELLS A WONDERFUL story in King Lear (my favorite Shakespearean tragedy) that should show what I mean when I say that philosophy is "perfectly ordinary."

In the opening scene we find King Lear dividing his kingdom between his three daughters. Before he reveals which portion of his kingdom will be hers, each daughter is instructed to tell her father how much she loves him.

The first daughter gives a very long, flowery speech. The next daughter outdoes the first with an even fancier one. Then comes the third daughter, Cordelia's turn. She refuses to compete with her sisters. At first she says nothing at all; then, when her father insists, she says, "I love you according to my bond, no more and no less." Her modest, little response infuriates King Lear and sets the play in motion. At the end of the story, Cordelia is vindicated as the only daughter who truly loved her father.

What is important about this story is Cordelia's little response. She is a model for what philosophy and education try to do. Both philosophy and education, in their own ways, try to describe things by showing what they seem to be. The more descriptive you can be, the better. This is what is true in the cliché "A picture is worth a thousand words." The writing dictum "Show; don't tell." expresses the same sentiment and truth.

Description is on grand display in the art of kindergarten teaching. A great kindergarten teacher can describe things to young children in simple, vivid, lively, and clear— but perfectly ordinary—ways. If philosophers could be half as descriptive as an excellent kindergarten teacher, they would become far better philosophers. At the very least, people might understand them better.

Good philosophy and education both show things. Mediocre philosophy and education only say things. Bad philosophy and education accomplish neither.

Teaching follows the same guideline. Magnificent teaching has the philosophical and educational capacity to describe the thing that is being taught. Average teaching only does so occasionally. Poor teaching, hardly worthy of the name, drones on without describing anything.

Cordelia made a choice to describe her love for her father in a very sparse, direct, and ordinary way. This may strike you as odd or perhaps even disrespectful, as King Lear seemed to take it, but the beauty in Cordelia's reply lives in the bare honesty of her description. She was fearless. She told the truth, suspecting she would suffer because of it—and she did (her father disowned her).

Regardless of her fate, Cordelia did not want to receive an inheritance for posturing and giving overwrought, dishonest descriptions of true love. Cordelia's simplicity, like the magnificent kindergarten teacher, is an important exemplar for philosophy and education.

"I love you according to my bond, no more and no less." This is what philosophy and education set out to do: To show things as they are, as best they can. No more and no less. And there is always more and less to be shown. This restless philosophical and educational project is always a work of art, striving for harmony, attunement, and balance.

When you go about talking, reading, writing, and thinking, strive to be like Cordelia. Be descriptive. Show more than you say.

When you wonder what to read for, read for what is there. Read for the truth! No more and no less. When you listen to a lecture or watch a movie, don't search for anything other than what is there, even if what is there is best described by referring to what is not there. When you ask a question, press an argument, or make a comment, attend to the descriptive task as best you can.

There are many ways to be descriptive, far more than I can name here. Good examples are very effective. Finely tuned arguments can show many things. Close, detailed observational accounts often work, too. Thought experiments can sometimes express something in vivid detail. Finding an exception or a counterfactual will many times offer clarity to a description. Considering objections and possible problems, even if you disagree with them, adds rigor and credibility to your description. And more. No matter what your route or strategy is, all descriptions must be rooted in a heartfelt attempt to show something. Show. Don't just tell. Show more than you say. At minimum, you must ensure that you are saying something and at least trying to show it, too. Regardless of execution, something should be at stake in your description. Some thing. A thing. More than just words.

‡

An exercise and a question: Describe a material thing you can observe directly—e.g., an object like a chair or an apple or a coin or your own fingernail—in as much detail as you can from the angle you see it. Write your description of the thing as a painter might paint it or a photographer might photograph it. Edit the prose as needed and condense it into one typed page. How does describing a material thing compare and contrast to a description, like Cordelia's, of true love?

# 6

# THINGS

PHILOSOPHY AND EDUCATION DESCRIBE things. What is a thing? This is not complicated to understand in a preliminary way, although it is nearly impossible to answer in an exhaustive way. Try thinking about it this way: A thing is something. Anything, really. Whatever impression comes to your physical eyes or your mind's eye is a thing. Even things you cannot see or imagine, things you are blind to, are things, too. Everything we can speak of or think about is, in some sense, a thing. And, insofar as a thing is something or anything, it cannot be nothing: it is something instead of nothing.

Anything is something: if this is true, then a thing cannot be nothing. A philosophy or education of nothing is nihilistic. And nihilism (nothingness) is antithetical to philosophy, education, and life itself—unless we consider nothingness itself as a thing, which is a different issue entirely.

The question now becomes how: how do we describe things? How do we show them? What tools do we use?

‡

Do some metaphysics: The word 'metaphysics' refers to questions and concerns related to what a thing is and why there is something instead of nothing. Another word for this kind of study is 'ontology,' which refers to the study of being. This is often related to another term, 'existentialism,' that refers generally to the way of being we experience as persons. One basic, but useful, way to think about what a thing is is by grouping things into two lists or columns: Things that exist and things that do not exist. Give it a try. Make two groups of words that refer to things that, on the one hand, exist, and, on the other hand, don't exist. Then think about it. You're doing metaphysics!

# 7

# LANGUAGE

THERE ARE MANY, MANY tools we can use to describe things. Musicians use musical instruments, painters use brushes and paint, sculptors use chisels and stone. Language is the tool that philosophers and educators normally use to describe things through speaking and writing. Whether they realize it or not, they also use other tools, too: their bodies, attitude, tone and sounds, and more. Nonetheless, their language is key. But be careful, very careful! Language is a tricky and often imprecise tool. It can create all kinds of confusions.

Remember this: the *tools* for description-making are not the same as the *things* that the tools are attempting to describe.

When I show you something using a tool—like a guitar resonating a minor chord; a paintbrush loaded with thick, royal-blue paint; a fine-point chisel on milky white marble; the keyboard I'm using to type these letters, words, and sentences—you cannot confuse the *tool* I am using with the *thing* I am trying to show by using said tool.

There is a difference between a word and the thing that a word is trying to describe. There may be a resemblance in your mind, but resemblance is not equivalence. There is a difference between a chaotic drum solo that sounds like a stampede and cows stampeding through your campground. There is a difference between a painting of a trout stream and a clear, ice-cold stream you are fly-fishing in. There is a difference between Michelangelo's Pieta and a mother holding the corpse of her dead son. A word is not the same thing as the thing to which it refers, even if it is beautiful, evocative, and apt.

Everyone knows there is a difference between a thing's name and the thing the name is describing. If you know languages, big words, and fancy names but know nothing about things, then you know nothing at all—nothing, that is, besides languages, big words, and fancy names.

Materially speaking, language is made of words just as words are made of letters and letters are made of shape and color. Since words are the descriptive tools for naming, names are not the same as the things they attempt to describe.

Yes, names—and all other aspects of language, like syntax and grammar—are "things" in a certain sense. But they are only things in *that* way, when they are self-referential, when they refer to themselves. For instance, the word 'words' is a five-letter term that can be used to refer to all word-things that collectively build language. But the word 'word' in its barest material reality is just a series of four shapes, rendered in color, sitting together on a horizontal plane, that can be used to describe itself and other words, like 'milk' and 'factory.'

Imagine naming your child "Name," or being named "Name" yourself. "Hello, my name is Name." It may sound silly, but it shows what I am trying to say. My name, "Sam," is not me; it is not who I am. My name is a word that refers to me, not the word 'me,' the person who writes to you right now.

What I am getting at is this: you should be able to tell the difference between the word 'dog' and a dog walking down the street.

Notice, look closely: 'dog' is a word, a shape really—composed of three letters that are formed, in this font, with four circular shapes, the first three in a horizontal row, the fourth hanging below the last one, with a vertical line shooting up from the first one and a tiny horizontal line pointing to the East from the last one's topmost circle—but a dog walking down the street is a thing.

One more example: the English alphabet has twenty-six letters, but the word 'alphabet' only has eight letters—or seven if we don't count the repetition of the letter 'a.' Regardless, the difference between the word 'alphabet' and the thing, the twenty-six-lettered English alphabet, is undeniable and the two should not be confused with each other.

Do not mistake words for things, unless you mean to focus on the things that words are, like I did in the previous examples. (The exercise of describing language is what "philosophy of language" does.) Always ask what thing any given word is attempting to describe when it is not obvious to you. Do not begin anything else until this is as clear as possible.

This is why words are important: they are your instrument—your guitar, your paintbrush, your chisel. Use them well. And remember, there is nothing about any given word that is required to describe any particular thing. Many words (like the word 'bat') are used to describe many different things, especially when put into larger or smaller semantic contexts, usages, and conversations.

For instance: my sons use the word 'dog' to refer to a push on the swing set. A "super dog" refers to a big push, and a "slippery dog" refers to a push that makes you fall off and get hurt. "Daddy, will you give me a super dog, please? Not a slippery dog!" They also refer to twisting the swing like a corkscrew and spinning around by using the word 'whizz.' "Look at me! I'm gonna do a GIANT whizz!" We do this sort of thing all the time. Words are flexible, so we should not assume that the thing they refer to is static or fixed.

Enough about words and language. Enough about tools. What do these descriptions amount to? More importantly, what do philosophy and education amount to? This is just another way of asking why you should take this seriously. Why should anyone take philosophy and education seriously? What do they offer in return?

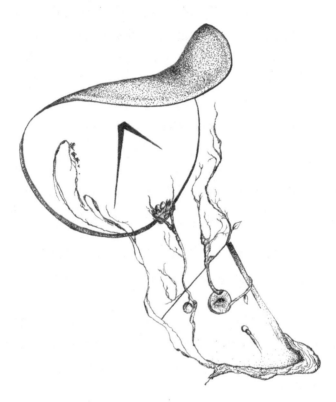

‡

An exercise (and a hint): In the simplest and most basic way possible, use words to describe the difference between the following two things in brackets: this [ ...... ] and this [ a six-dotted line ]. (Here's a hint: Just describe what each thing looks like, its shape and color. Nothing more, nothing less.)

# 8

## COURAGE

FIRST, LET'S BE CLEAR about what philosophy and education do not amount to, what they do not offer in return: philosophy and education do not amount to grades, diplomas, credentials, or other byproducts of schooling.

It is common for students to man an effort something—including, but not limited to, reading this book or other assigned readings, writing a paper, or attending a class session—for the sole purpose of trying to get a high grade or to avoid a low one. People oftentimes attend classes only to secure a certain grade. Otherwise they would gladly skip.

In many colleges and universities, there are students who care more about being on the list of some person they hardly know (the Dean), based on three numbers and a decimal point (their grade point average), than they do about anything else related to their studies. In fact, students often become "students" in the first place for the same reasons. Surely you've at least heard of such students, if you're not one yourself. Sadly, these people have been conditioned to feel and act this way in previous schooling institutions and elsewhere, too. Many of us have internalized the motivational rewards and external prizes offered by institutions. But there has never been an infant who cared about grades, awards, or credentials.

Students like these are often unmotivated except by a sense of entrapment, a feeling that they must go to school and get good grades in order to get a respectable job, good reviews and promotions, a pay raise for having an advanced degree, so on and so forth—the alienation that comes from fleeing alienation, from trying to avoid disappointing family and friends.

Doing something out fear of failure can never yield a true success or full accomplishment because, after the glamor and glitz is worn by time, the fear will remain or return. Nonetheless, this is not a zero sum game, there is hope within tragedy, motivations are never as pure as we'd like them to be and do not rule the day. There no more reason to fear being afraid than there is to be afraid in the first place.

To be a student is simply to study, and students worthy of the name study *beautifully*, for the sake of study itself. While the object of studies can vary, love for the rigor of study—curiosity, attention, memory, and imagination—is the same throughout.

Of course students who attend a school that assigns grades should to some degree want to get good grades. They should obviously not want to get bad ones. However, you should not confuse this institutionalized process of grade-getting, school-going, degree-worshipping, and job-seeking, and fear and shame that can go along with it, with what philosophy and education have to offer you through study.

I am not teaching this class (nor am I writing this book) to provide you with any of those things, even as I recognize that they are not altogether trivial or unimportant to you or me. We could just as easily do this sort of work in my living room or a public library for no credit or credentials. Anywhere, really. After all, even the work of the school is often done best when school is not in session, at home, at the café, the park or library. To study outside the school is not the exception; it is the overwhelming norm. Philosophy and education predate formalized compulsory schooling by millennia. Formal schooling does not have a monopoly on the study of philosophy or education. Most philosophy and education take place outside of formal schools, in the only school humans have universally attended throughout history: the world.

Again: philosophy and education do not amount to grades or any equivalent external reward. Still, you are probably keenly aware—for better and worse reasons—that there is a grade attached to most classes, including this one, but that isn't the primary issue. If you write, read, and attend class solely to squeeze out a respectable grade, you will probably struggle in ways that those who write, read, and attend for other, better reasons do not. If you are serious, you will do the work for its own sake. Recall running: serious marathon runners do not run for money or prizes alone; they run to run. Likewise, I know of no serious kindergarten teachers who entered the profession for money or prestige. They teach with the dignity of artists: their art—the art of teaching—is its own reward.

This is why the professionalization of sports often degrades and perverts the art and joy of sporting by turning it into something it is not: a business, a science, a competition for rewards and profits. The same goes for many other things.

The problem with grades, credentials, and formal schooling in general, is that it often generates a culture and mentality of fear, distrust, and paranoia. Worst of all, it erodes what is truly worthwhile, replacing what is serious with a joke. There is no hope in this approach. It would be like trying to fall in love and get married in order to pay lower taxes: taxes are an inescapable reality for many of us, but they are no reason to fall in love; lower tax rates simply come as happy accidents. Even if tax rates rose, true love would still overcome. Likewise, good grades come as happy accidents, too.

Philosophy and education focus on being descriptive and cannot be distracted from this task. Recall Cordelia: she didn't worry about the possible fallout from her honest description. She didn't let the assignment or the test get in the way of the real task at hand.

She told the truth.

Read for the truth. Write and speak to show what seems true. Ask questions to get at what might be true. Attend classes to seek the truth. Do not settle for shallow, impoverished grades and cheap, degrading rewards. Do not be bullied or bribed into philosophy. Do not take education courses to simply beg for more money or prestige or a job promotion. Do not live in fear. Be brave like Cordelia. Philosophy and education require courage.

‡

A confession and a question: In my own life, courage is rare. I don't think I am a coward outright, but I am certainly not courageous. I prefer to be comfortable, and seeking comfort often leads to outright cowardice. Showing courage would require me to do things I don't like to do, to seek out and embrace all sorts of discomfort and even suffering. So I tend to spend a great deal of effort trying to figure out ways to escape the rigors of courage. How about you?

‡

(In the section to follow, I will move from priming to painting, from philosophizing and educating with primer to philosophizing and educating with paint.)

# 9

# KNOWING AND
# UNDERSTANDING

WITH COURAGE, WITH THE tough, loving attitude that genuine seriousness brings, philosophy and education yield knowledge. Yet, as we
will see, knowledge itself is not enough. We
must *understand*.

The English word 'knowledge' does not
always refer to just one thing. There are at
least two different ways in which we can know
something. They are not mutually exclusive.
They do not always happen apart from each
other. But there is an important, obvious difference between the "knowledge" I have of my
social security number, on the one hand, and
the "knowledge" I have of my children, or myself, on the other.

Google is full of information, but it has
no wisdom of its own. A person who is full
of information is not necessarily full of wisdom. To be informed is not the same thing as

to be wise. To win at games like Jeopardy and Trivial Pursuit does not require wisdom, it only requires information.

Trivia certainly has its place, but one should not confuse trivial information with wisdom. In fact, a wise person may not always be well informed and may even be misinformed in certain respects. This is why so many informed people are so dreadfully unwise and many wise people are often underinformed. The sage, the person of wisdom, might understand, even if she does not know.

This is also why many people who are well schooled are so poorly educated. After the 2012 summer shooting in Aurora, Colorado, many wondered, "How could such a bright, schooled person, a Ph.D. student in neuroscience, commit a mass murder?"

We live in the Information Age, the age of Google and Wikipedia. Yet, even though information and data abound, wisdom is in short supply. We seem to know-about everything but actually know very little. Knowledge and its progenies, like science and technology, proliferate, but understanding seems scarce as ever.

After all, no one wants to be consoled by a rocket scientist when they are dying—unless your lover or family member happens, coincidentally, to be a rocket scientist. We would rather have our loved ones at our deathbed. We want empathy, not genius. Compassion, not erudition. While we are more sophisticated than ever at curing disease and illness, all of that progress is incapable of consoling those who are suffering and dying.

For these reasons and more, you should recognize and try to understand the difference between information-knowledge and wisdom-knowledge, between knowing-about something and knowing something, the limits of knowledge and the excess of understanding.

There is a famous saying attributed to Socrates: "Know thyself." Know. Thy. Self. What does the word 'know' refer to here? Is it enough to know-about one's self, to be merely informed about one's self? Can one know all the information of a "self"—physical details, family tree, likes and dislikes, and more—and claim to truly know that self?

No.

In order to know someone, including yourself, you must possess more than information about that self. When it comes to self-knowledge, information can never replace wisdom. And wisdom requires understanding.

In Spanish there are two words for the English expression "to know": 'saber' and 'conocer.' Many other languages have the same two forms of words for knowing ('wissen' and 'kennen' in German, 'savoir' and 'connaître' in French). Allow me to describe what each word refers to, as an attempt to show what I've said:

Saber—To saber something is to know about it in a cold, thin, objective way. When someone asks me where the bathroom is, assuming that I actually "know" where the bathroom is, my response giving directions to the bathroom—"in the very back of the store, by the cereal aisle, you'll see the sign"—shows that I saber where the bathroom is.

Or, when someone else asks me whether I "know" what the word 'platypus' is in Spanish and I reveal that I do not "know," I am indicating that I do not saber the Spanish equivalent for the English word 'platypus.' In the first instance (the bathroom) I was informed. In the second (the word 'platypus') I was uninformed.

Conocer—To conocer something is to know about it in a warm, thick, subjective way. When someone asks me if I "know" my mother, my affirmative response shows that I conocer my mother. (To only know-about her would be to not know her; "I never really knew her, I only know-about her," I might say.)

Similarly, if someone asks me whether I know who I am, and I reveal that I do not "know," I am indicating that I do not conocer myself, that I do not conocer who I am. This sense of knowing is wisdom that reaches beyond knowledge and enters the realm of understanding.

There is nothing about the way I saber that can substitute for the way I conocer. No one could confuse how a lover knows her beloved with how she knows-about the characters in a romantic novel.

To know something in a saber way is important; it is not to be disregarded or thrown out. But philosophy and education, like a strong ocean undercurrent, always pull us in deeper than saber, into the conocer ways of knowing and even beyond knowledge, into understanding.

Our understanding of something might begin with saber knowledge on the surface, but philosophy and education call us further into the wisdom of conocer knowledge and the understanding that lies below the surface of knowledge.

Philosophy and education call us into the abyss of wisdom. This happens because we are drawn to know in warmer, thicker, deeper, and fuller ways. To understand. "I don't really know what you're going through right now, but I understand nonetheless."

We all desire more than facts, names, and titles. We will starve if only fed the trivia of

Google or Wikipedia. We hunger and thirst for wisdom and understanding. We want to be more than merely informed: we want to be courageous and wise. Like Cordelia: to understand.

What takes us from information to wisdom? How does one understand? What could possibly carry us to the nurturing bosom of wisdom and the fruit of understanding? And what does understanding offer beyond itself?

Love.

We are drawn by love towards wisdom into understanding, drawn beyond information, grades, credentials, paychecks, "success," and shallower notions of philosophy and education. We are carried by love to the fountain of wisdom with hope that it, like art, will yield its own reward: love for love.

‡

Some thoughts and an exercise: Think about something you know in a *saber* way, another thing you know in a *conocer* way, and something else you want to *understand*. In a short paragraph, try to describe each one separately.

# 10

# BEING IN LOVE

PHILOSOPHY IS LOVE OF wisdom. The love that this love begets is education. No more and no less. In the end, philosophy and education are understood, not known. Understanding is beyond the scope of knowledge because it requires more than knowing, it requires being—being in love.

When we drink from the font of wisdom we are filled with more than wisdom itself: we acquire understanding. By understanding, we become more than wise philosophers and sage educators. We become persons; we are personalized. We realize that we desire more than wisdom, more than to move beyond information and forms of knowledge into understanding. Persons fundamentally desire and require love: to love and be loved. It is better to be in love than to be wise. Without love, there is no understanding. Without love, there is nothing.

True wisdom will not settle for itself. A wise person is not content to be wise. My late Grandpa Rocha—to and for whom this book is dedicated—understood and lived this thoroughly. He was not particularly well schooled, but he was deeply educated. Like Abraham Lincoln, he only attended a formal school until the third grade.

He was a master storyteller. Tales told and retold fill my imagination and heart to this day. He also taught me elementary mathematics, penmanship, and how to speak and read Spanish. Most of all, he taught me about life and love and simple happiness and forgiveness and the value of hard work. During his last days my Grandpa Rocha taught me about the dignity of suffering; he showed me how to die a beautiful death.

He was a wise man, a man of incredible understanding. But I will not remember him for his wisdom or even his understanding: I will cherish him for his love. His love was, is, and will continue to be sufficient. Because of his love, he has been, and always will be, one of my greatest teachers.

This is where philosophy and education end and life begins: in love. This is also where philosophy and education begin anew.

Love alone is necessary and sufficient for all things. Everything else is secondary. Without love, this primer, this class, and this life are senseless, futile, and in vain. Be in love. Dwell in it, and you will surely be primed for whatever comes your way.

‡

One final question: What can be said of that which has been *shown*?

# SUGGESTIONS FOR FURTHER STUDY

Plato. *Meno.*

Augustine. *Confessions.*

Dante. *La Vita Nuova,*

Shakespeare. *King Lear.*

Jean-Jacque Rousseau. *Emile.*

Herman Melville. *Bartleby the Scribner.*

Mark Twain. *Adventures of Huckleberry Finn.*

Leo Tolstoy. *The Death of Ivan Ilyich.*

William James. *Talks to Teachers on Psychology.*

Pablo Neruda. *Twenty Love Poems and a Song of Despair.*

Rainer Maria Rilke. *Letters to a Young Poet.*

John Dewey. *Experience and Education.*

John Coltrane. *A Love Supreme.* (music)

Ray Monk. *The Duty of Genius.*

Margaret Edson. *Wit.* (film)

Terrance Malick. *The Tree of Life.* (film)

Made in the USA
Coppell, TX
09 May 2022

77560304R00049